GCSE ARABIC
ESSENTIAL
VOCABULARY LIST

ISBN 9953-29-632-4

Published by:

LINKS PUBLISHING
United Kingdom
P.O. Box: 145
Stockport
SK7 IWJ
Tel: 0161-2858561
Fax: 0161-2858561
e-mail: zeina@khavat.co.uk

Distributed by:

Arab Scientific Publishers
Beirut, Lebanon
Tel: 00961-1-786233
Fax: 00961-1-786230

GCSE ARABIC

ESSENTIAL

VOCABULARY LIST

An Arabic-English vocabulary list arranged by topic and required for the GCSE examination

Zeina Debs Khayat

(PGCE) Post Graduate Certificate in Education

Illustrations By

Leila Awwa Al-Waraa

LINKS Publishing   **Arab Scientific Publishers**

Contents

Foreword

This Arabic General Certificate of Secondary Education (GCSE) essential vocabulary list is a supplementary tool to aid students intending to take the GCSE Arabic language examination.

All the words are listed by topic, thus covering the main areas required in the four skills (reading, writing, listening, and speaking) for the GCSE examination.

The last pages of this book link key words to pictures in order to further help the student recall essential vocabulary.

This book will hopefully aid students in their examination as well as to acquire a basic knowledge of the Arabic modern language.

AT HOME AND ABROAD

On The Right	على اليمين
On The Left	على اليسار
Abroad	خارج البلد
Reception	استقبال
Welcomes	يرحّب/ترحّب
Activities	نشاطات
Train	قطار
Airport	مطار
Notices	يلاحظ/تلاحظ
Loves	يحب
Ticket	تذكرة
Return Ticket	تذكرة ذهاب وإياب
One Way Ticket	تذكرة ذهاب
Fun	تسلية
Camera	آلة تصوير
Named	يسمّى/تسمّى
Bus Stop	موقف باص
Lift	مصعد

Arrives	يصل/تصل
Lands (the airplane)	تهبط (الطائرة)
At the beach	على شاطئ البحر
Traveler	مسافر
Youth hostel	نزل للشباب
Expressway	طريق سريع
Heavy rain	وابل من المطر
Aircraft	طائرة
Luggage	أمتعة سفر
Toilet	حمّام، دورة مياه، مرحاض
Balcony	بلكون، شرفة
Suburb	ضاحية
Bank	بنك، مصرف
Boat	قارب
Building	عمارة
Beautiful	جميل، رائع
Library	مكتبة
Happy stay	إقامة سعيدة
Good trip	رحلة سعيدة

Fog	ضباب
Lost property office	مكتب الأشياء المفقودة
Countryside	ريف
Coach	حافلة
Crossroads	مفترق طرق
Postcard	بطاقة بريدية
Shopping center	مركز تسوّق
City center	مركز المدينة
Temperature	حرارة
Bakery	مخبز
Castle	قلعة
Hot	حارّ
Railway	سكة حديد
Expensive	غالي
Horse	حصان، فرس
Sky	سماء
Traffic	السير، حركة مرور السيارات
Climate	مناخ، طقس، جوّ
Hill	تلّ

Camp	مخيّم
Police station	مركز شرطة، مخفر شرطة
Full, reserved	مليء، محجوز
Sports center	مركز رياضي
Dials	يطلب/تطلب رقم الهاتف
Drives	يقود/تقود
Safe deposit	خزانة الودائع
Continues	يستمر
Conductor	مفتّش التذاكر
Relation	علاقة، رابطة
Beach	شاطئ
Berth, mooring	مرسى
Cloudy	غائم، ملبّد بالغيوم
Takes off	يقلع/تقلع
Describes	يصف/تصف
Empties a suitcase	يفرّغ محتويات حقيبة
Forbidden	ممنوع
Steps	درجات
Tomorrow	غداً

Area, county	منطقة، مقاطعة
Bulletin	نشرة
Leaves	يترك/تترك
Games	ألعاب
Overlooks	يطلّ/تطلّ على، يشرف
Customs	جمارك، جمرك
Crosses	يعبر/تعبر
Straight	مستقيم
Temple	معبد
Mosque	مسجد، جامع
Church	كنيسة
Crowded	ازدحام، مزدحم
Location, site	موقع
Breaks down	يتعطّل/تتعطّل
Place	مكان
Boring	مملّ
Petrol	بنزين
Turn, (period)	دور
Star	نجم

Trip, walk, outing	نزهة
Excuse me!	عفواً، عذراً
Moon	قمر
Camp	مخيّم
Gets to know	يتعرّف على
Fills up	يملأ تماماً
Packs, fasten	يحزم/تحزم، يربط
Farm	مزرعة
Celebrates	يحتفل بِ
Welcomes	يرحب بِ
Traffic light	إشارة المرور
(Application) form	استمارة
Son	ابن
Fountain	نافورة
Scarf	وشاح
Cold	بارد
Border	حدود، حد
Station	محطة
Bus stop	موقف الحافلات، الباصات

14

Stops the car	يوقف/توقف السيارة
Policeman	شرطي
Ticket office	شباك تذاكر
Citizen	مواطن
Lives	يسكن/تسكن
Historical	تاريخي
Town hall	دار بلدية
Complete	كامل، مكتمل
Comprehensive	شامل، مشتمل
Industrial	صناعي
Park	منتزه
Zoo	حديقة حيوانات
Holiday	يوم عطلة
Public holiday	عطلة عامة
Newspaper kiosk	كشك (صحف ومجلات)
Torch	مشعل (مصباح)
Slow	بطيء
Free	حر
For hire	للإيجار، للتأجير

Far	بعيد
Rents	يستأجر/تستأجر
Shop	حانوت، دكان
Market	سوق
Walks	يمشي/تمشي
Bad	رديء، سيّئ
Best regards	أطيب التحيّات
Sea	بحر
Thank you	شكراً
Weather forecast	تنبّؤات جوية
Metre	متر
Noon	ظهر
Mountain	جبل
Rides	يركب/تركب
Engine	محرك
Motorcycle	درّاجة ناريّة
Dies	يموت/تموت
Mosquito	بعوضة
Museum	متحف

Snow	ثلج
Unsuitable for drinking	غير صالح للشرب
South	جنوب
West	غرب
East	شرق
North	شمال
Cloud	غيمة
Tourist office	مكتب سياحة
Storm	عاصفة
Can opener	فتّاحة علب
Bottle opener	فتّاحة زجاجات
Palace	قصر
Parcel, parcels	طرد، طرود
Umbrella	مظلة
Car Park	موقف سيارات، للسيارات
Public garden	حديقة عامة
Passes	يمُرّ/تمر
Country	بلد، وطن
Beautiful scene	منظر جميل

English	العربية
Film	فلم
Loses	يخسر، يفقد/تخسر، تفقد
Driving license	رخصة قيادة
Person	شخص
Identity card	هوية (شخصية)
Foot	قدم
Pedestrian	ماش (مشاة)
Swimming pool	مسبح
Beautiful	فاتن، رائع، جميل
square	ميدان
Beach	شاطئ
Rains	تمطر (السماء)
Rain	مطر
Bridge	جسر
Door	باب
Post office	مكتب بريد
For drinking	للشرب
Near	قرب
Next to	قريب من، بجانب

Pavement	رصيف
Neighborhood	حيّ، حارة
Receives	يستلم/تستلم
Thanks	يشكر/تشكر
Fills	يملأ/تملأ
Meets	يقابل/تقابل
Information	معلومات
Reserves	يحجز/تحجز
Delay	تأخير
Roundabout	دوّار
Walks	يسير/تسير
Main road	طريق رئيسي
Road	طريق
Called	يسمى/تسمى
Sand	رمل
Suitcase, a case, a bag	حقيبة
Sleeping bag	حقيبة نوم
Season	فصل
Waiting room	غرفة انتظار

Playroom	غرفة ألعاب
Unleaded	خالٍ من الرصاص
Stops	يقف/تقف
Bathes	يستحم/تستحم، يغتسل
Sunbathes	يتشمس/تتشمس
Available	متاح، موجود
Safety	أمن، سلامة
Stays, remins	يبقى
One way	اتجاه واحد
Please	رجاءً
Sun	شمس
Suffers, endures	يعاني/تعاني
Lime	كلس
Stadium	ملعب، مدرج
Stops	يوقف/توقف، يتوقف/تتوقف
In addition	بالإضافة
Weather	جو، حالة الجو
Tour	جولة
Tower	برج

Turns	يدير/تدير
Foreward	إلى الأمام
Trip	سفرة، رحلة
Calm	هادئ
Public transport	وسيلة نقل عامة
Crosses	يعبر/تعبر
Break, holiday	عطلة، إجازة
Cow	بقرة
Bicycle	دراجة هوائية
Wind	ريح
Towards	باتجاه
Town	مدينة
Quick	سريع
Looks	ينظر/تنظر
Car	سيارة
Flies	يطير/تطير
Wants	يريد/تريد
View	منظر
Sleeping car	عربة نوم

Pedestrian area	منطقة مشاة
Train	قطار

EDUCATION, TRAINING AND EMPLOYMENT

Helps	يساعد/تساعد
Likes	يحب/تحب
Leader	قائد
Announces	يعلن/تعلن
Calls for, sends for	يستدعي/تستدعي
Learns	يتعلم/تتعلم
Practises	يتمرن، يتدرب، يمارس/تمارس
Training	تمرين، تدريب
Sit	اجلس
Coach, bus	حافلة، باص
Future	مستقبل
Building	بناية، عمارة
Speaks	يتحدث/تتحدث
Good	جيد
Postbox	صندوق بريد
Works	يعمل/تعمل
Office	مكتب
Exercise book	دفتر تمارين

Calculator	حاسبة
Profession	مهنة
School bag	حقيبة مدرسية
Taxi driver	سائق سيارة أجرة
Looks for	يبحث/تبحث عن
Unemployment	بطالة
Keyboard	لوحة مفاتيح
Hairdresser	مصففة شعر ، حلاقة
School	مدرسة
Starts	يبدأ/تبدأ
Accountant	محاسب
Advises	ينصح، يشير/تشير
Telephone call	مكالمة هاتفية
Post	بريد
Lesson	درس، حصة
Tennis	كرة المضرب
Dinner	عشاء
Art	فن، فنون
Draws	يرسم/ترسم

Hates	يكره/تكره
House chore	واجب بيتي
Difficult	صعب
Qualified	مؤهل
Headmaster	مدير مدرسة
Floppy disk	قرص مرن
Discusses	يتباحث، يتناقش/تتناقش
Exchanges	يتبادل/تتبادل
Screen	شاشة
School	مدرسة
Nursery	روضة أطفال
Primary school	مدرسة ابتدائية
Secondary school	مدرسة ثانوية
Student	تلميذ/طالب
Employee	موظف
Businessman	صاحب عمل
Timetable	جدول زمني
Boring	ممل
Studies	دراسة، دراسات

Teaching	تدريس
Sends	يرسل/ترسل
Physical education	تربية رياضية
Student	طالب
Studies	يدرس/تدرس
Example	مثال
Sent	مرسل
Experienced	ذو خبرة
Explains	يشرح/تشرح، يفسر
Easy	سهل
Postman	ساعي البريد
Finishes a course of study	يكمل/تكمل دورة دراسية
Gains Professional experience	يحصل على خبرة مهنية
Wrong	خطأ
Ends	ينهي/تنهي
Obtains, receives	يحصل/تحصل على
Eraser	ممحاة
Summer holiday	عطلة صيفية

Play room	صالة ألعاب
Hour	ساعة
Businessman	رجل أعمال
Typewriter	آلة طباعة
Types	يطبع/تطبع
Blade	شفرة
Architect, engineer	مهندس
Interesting	مشوق، ملفت للنظر
Open	مفتوح
Day	يوم
Laboratory	مختبر
Language	لغة
Letter	رسالة
Step, grade, degree	درجة
Book	كتاب
Pound Sterling	جنيه إسترليني
School	مدرسة
Builder	بنّاء
Shop	حانوت، دكّان، مخزن

Tape recorder	آلة تسجيل صوت
Video recorder	آلة تسجيل تلفازية
Television	تلفاز
Low income	واطي الدخل (ذو دخل متدنٍّ)
Subject	موضوع، مادّة دراسية
Mechanic	ميكانيكي
Doctor	طبيب
E-mail	بريد إلكتروني
Underground	قطار أنفاق
Instructor, supervisor	موجِّه، مشرف
Word	كلمة
Mark	علامة، درجة
Stay on line	ابقَ على الخط
Worker	عامل
Busy, occupied, engaged	مشغول
Computer	حاسوب
Forgets	ينسى/تنسى
Trousers	سروال، بنطلون
Paper	ورق

President	رئيس
Lunchtime	وقت الغداء
Paid	مدفوع
Pays	يدفع
Loses	يفقد، يخسر
Allows	يسمح/تسمح
Looks for a job	يطلب عمل أو وظيفة، يسعى/تسعى إلى عمل
Favorite	مفضّل
Prefers	يفضّل
Teacher	مدرّس، معلّم
Program	برنامج
Walks	ماش (على الأقدام)، يمشي/تمشي
Presents	يقدم/تقدم
Geography	جغرافيا
English	إنكليزي
French	فرنسي
Music lesson class	فصل موسيقى
History	تاريخ

Mathematics	رياضيّات
Physics	فيزياء
Biology	علم الأحياء
Chemistry	كيمياء
Plan	خطّة
Break	(فرصة)، وقت استراحة
Ruler	مسطرة
Appointment	موعد
Back to school	العودة إلى المدرسة
Repeats	يعيد، يكرر/تكرر
Answering machine	آلة تسجيل المكالمات الهاتفيّة
Answers	يجيب/تجيب
Summary	ملخّص، موجز
Detention	احتجاز
Meeting	اجتماع
Rucksack, backpack	حقيبة الظهر
Applies, Submits an application	يتقدم/تتقدم بطلب
Salary	معاش، راتب

Wage	أجر
Classroom, class	صف، فصل دراسي
Staff room	غرفة المدرسين
Memorizes	يحفظ/تحفظ عن ظهر قلب
Learns	يتعلّم
Pronounces	يتهجى
Spells	يلفظ
Waiter	خادم مطعم
First year	السنة الأولى
Rings (the bell)	يقرع (الجرس)
Teacher	مدرّس، أستاذ
Pen	قلم حبر
Board	لوح
Pencil Sharpener	مبراة
Types	يطبع على الآلة الكاتبة
Talks on the phone	يكلم بالهاتف
Year thirteen/year seven	السنة الثالثة عشر
Sport ground	ملعب الرياضة
Stamp	طابع (بريدي)

Works	يعمل/تعمل
Period	مدة
Pencil case	مقلمة، حافظة أقلام
University	جامعة
Factory	معمل، مصنع
Assistant, employee	مساعد، موظف
Sales	مبيعات
Old	قديم
Car	سيارة

HEALTH AND FITNESS

Improves	يتحسن/تتحسن
Stomachache	(مصاب) بألم المعدة
Earache	(مصاب) بألم الأذن
Inflammation	التهاب
Throat	الحنجرة
Headache	(مصاب) بالصداع
Nauseous	يشعر/تشعر بالغثيان
Has Backache	(مصاب) بألم الظهر
Wounded	مجروح
Has Toothache	(مصاب) بألم الأسنان
Harms himself	يسبب الأذى لنفسه، يؤذي نفسه
Pill, tablet	قرص (دواء)
Sleeps	ينام/تنام
Fever	حمى
Smokes	يدخن/تدخن
Mouth	فم
Strong	قوي
Cold	زكام

Nurse	ممرض، ممرضة
Man	رجل
Patient	مريض
Illness	مرض
Doctor	طبيب
Woman	امرأة
Handkerchief	منديل
Nose	أنف
Eye	عين
Prescription	وصفة طبية
Stings	يلسع/تلسع
Sting	لسعة
Carries	يحمل/تحمل
Recipe	وصفة طهي
Appointment	موعد
Cold	برد
Healthy	صحي، متعاف
Rests	يستريح/تستريح
Sweet drink	شراب سكري

Head	رأس
Falls ill	يصاب/تصاب بالمرض، مريض
Coughs	يسعل/تسعل
Vegetarian	نباتي
Dentist	طبيب أسنان
Eyes	عيون

HOUSE, HOME AND DAILY ROUTINE

Old	مسن، كبير السن
The oldest	الأكبر سناً
Address	عنوان
Helps	يساعد/تساعد
Friendly	ودِّي
Hosts	يضيف/تضيف
Friendship	صداقة
Friend	صديق، صديقة
Love	حب
Loves	يحب/تحب
Pineapple	أناناس
Banana	موزة
Butter	زبدة
Beef	لحم بقر
Carrot	جزرة
Sultanas	زبيب
Cherries	كرز

Mushrooms	فطر
Chips	بطاطا مقلية
Cabbage	كرنب، لهانة
Cauliflower	قنبيط، قرنبيط
Lemon	ليمون
Jam	مربى
Fresh Vegetables	خضر طازجة
Sweet, pudding	حلوى
Cream	قشطة، قشدة
Strawberries	فراولة
Apple	تفّاحة
Turkey	ديك رومي
Mineral water	ماء معدني
Cheese	جبنة
Cake	كعكة
Chocolate drink	شراب شوكولاتة
Vegetables	خضر
Seafood	طعام بحري

Flour	طحين، دقيق
Cutlets	لحم أضلاع
Pork	لحم خنزير
White coffee	قهوة بالحليب
Frozen items, Foods	مثلّجات
Mustard	خردل
Lamb	خروف صغير
Egg	بيضة
Milk	حليب
Juice	عصير
Onion	بصل
Drink	شراب
Lemonade	ليمونادة
Food	طعام
Bread	خبز
Toasted bread	خبز محمّص
Fizzy orange drink	شراب فوّار بنكهة البرتقال
Pear	إجاص

Meat	لحم
Tomato	طماطم
Wine, alcohol	خمر، نبيذ، كحول
Vinegar	خل
Veal	لحم عجل
Tuna	سمك تونة
Tea	شاي
Bread and butter	خبز وزبدة
Sugar	سكر
Salt	ملح
Rice	أرز
Green salad	سلطة خضراء
Sausage	سجق
Grapes	عنب
Chicken	دجاج
Soup	حساء، شوربة
Potato	بطاطس
Pepper	فلفل

Fish	سمك
Plum	خوخ
Oil	زيت
Meal	وجبة
Light meal	وجبة خفيفة
Appetizers	مقبلات
Breakfast	فطور
Flat	شقة
Tree	شجرة
Cupboard	خزانة
Dish, plate	طبق، صحن
Heats	يسخن/تسخن
Gets hungry	يجوع/تجوع
Becomes cold	يبرد/تبرد
Drinks	يشرب/تشرب
Can	علبة صفيح
Enjoy your meal, drink	هنيئاً
Mouth	فم

Bottle	قنينة
Arm	ذراع
Office	مكتب
The smallest, the youngest	الأصغر
Coffee pot	إبريق قهوة
Sofa, armchair	أريكة
Duck	بطة
Giraffe	زرافة
Amount, quantity	مقدار، كمية
Chair	كرسي
Bedroom	غرفة نوم
Hot	ساخن
Orders	يأمر/تأمر
Relaxed, resting	مرتاح
Frozen	مجمدة، مجمد
Neck	رقبة
Cuts	يقطع/تقطع
Knife	سكين

Cover, quilt, blanket	لحاف، بطانية
Spoon	ملعقة
Spoonful	مقدار ملعقة
Kitchen	مطبخ
Cook	طباخ
Nutrition	غذاء
Nice, delicious, tasty	لذيذ
Age	سن
Dinner	عشاء
Finger	إصبع
Cooks	يطبخ/تطبخ
Washes the dishes	يغسل/تغسل الأطباق
Tidies the garden	يرتب/ترتب الحديقة
Makes the bed	يرتب/ترتب الفراش
Does the housework	يقوم/تقوم بالعمل المنزلي
Irons the clothes	يكوي/تكوي الملابس
Does the shopping	يشتري/تشتري الحاجيات المنزلية
Tired	تعبان، تعب

Armchair	كرسي بمساند
Window	شباك
Flower	زهرة، وردة
Fork	شوكة
Fresh	طازج
Fridge	ثلاجة
Stays in bed	يبقى/تبقى في الفراش
Gas	غاز
Knee	ركبة
Lives	يسكن، يعيش/تعيش
Man	رجل
Garden	حديقة
Sink	حوض غسيل
Dishwasher	غسالة صحون
Bed	فراش
Light	ضوء
Washing machine	غسالة ملابس
Hand	يد

House	بيت
Cooking pot	قدر طبخ
Morning	صباح
Mixes	يخلط/تخلط
Lays the table	يعد/تعد الطاولة، المائدة
Furniture	أثاث
Carpet	سجاد
Wall	حائط
Tablecloth	شرشف طاولة
Cleans	ينظف/تنظف
Ear	أذن
Pillow, cushion	وسادة
Bottle opener	فتّاحة قناني
Perfume, flavour	عطر، نكهة
Shares	يشارك/تشارك
Garden lawn	حشيش الحديقة
Loses	يخسر/تخسر
Glasses	نظارات

Room	غرفة
Foot	قدم
Cupboard	خزانة
Roof	سقف
Ground	أرض
Plant	نبتة
Plate	صحن
Frying pan	مقلاة
Door	باب
Dustbin	سلة مهملات، نفايات
Tidies	يرتب/ترتب
Razor	موسى
Returns home	يعود إلى المنزل
Stays	يبقى/تبقى
Alarm clock	ساعة بمنبه
Ground floor	طابق أرضي
Curtain	ستارة
Tap	حنفية

Grills	يشوي/تشوي
Dining room	غرفة طعام
Bathroom	حمام
Sitting room	غرفة جلوس
Spreads	يُفَرِّش
Goes to bed, sleeps	يذهب للفراش، ينام/تنام
Undresses	يخلع ثيابه/تخلع ثيابها
Washes oneself, bathes	يغتسل/تغتسل
Rises	ينهض/تنهض
Shaves	يحلق/تحلق
Wakes up	يستيقظ/تستيقظ
Serves	يخدم/تخدم
Dresses up	يرتدي/ترتدي، يلبس ثيابه
Evening	مساء
Dinner	عشاء
Studio	شقة مؤلفة من غرفة واحدة
Carpet	سجادة
Late	متأخر

Cup	كوب
Terrace, balcony	شرفة
Shy	خجول
Cork	سداد فليني
Roof	سقف
Works	يعمل/تعمل
Glass	زجاج
Serves food or drink	يسكب/تسكب، يسقي/تسقي
Hall	قاعة
Face	وجه
Voice	صوت
Toilets	دورة مياه

MEDIA, ENTERTAINMENT AND YOUTH CULTURE

News	أخبار
Adult, mature	بالغ
Actor/actress	ممثّل/ممثّلة
Amusement	تسلية
Trainer, coache	مدرّب
Ticket	تذكرة
Income	دخل، مداخيل
Belt	حزام
Hat	قبعة
Socks	جوارب
Shoes	أحذية
Shirt	قميص
Sleeve	كم
Scarf	وشاح
Gloves	قفازات
Skirt	تنورة
Swimming suit	لباس سباحة
Dress	فستان

Jacket	سترة
Shirt	بلوزة
Coat	معطف
Handbag	حقيبة يد
Trousers	بنطلون، سروال
Clothes	ثياب
Cotton	قطن
Leather	جلد
Woollen	صوفي
Track suit	بدلة رياضية
(Fashion) model	عارض أزياء، عارضة أزياء
Fashion	موضة
Decoration	زينة
Dressed up, clothed	مرتد لملابسه
Famous	شهير
Channel	قناة
Song	أغنية
Sings	يغني/تغني
Singer	مغني

Starts	يبدأ/تبدأ
Costs	يكلف/تكلف
Television program	برنامج تلفازي
Entrance	مدخل
Student	طالب
Fan	مروحة
Sides with, takes side of	متعصب لِ
Comedy movie	فلم هزلي، كوميدي
Romantic movie	فلم عاطفي
Cartoons	رسوم متحركة
Documentary (film)	وثائقي
Adventure movie	فلم مغامرات
Horror movie	فلم مرعب
Detective movie	فلم بوليس سري
Ends	ينهي/تنهي
Reading	قراءة
Competition	مسابقة
Newspaper	جريدة
Play	تمثيلية

Theatre	مسرح
Game	لعبة
Seat	مقعد
Mobile telephone	هاتف نقال، جوّال
Price	سعر، ثمن
Reduced	مخفض
Reduction	تخفيض
Reserves	يحجز/تحجز
Lipstick	أحمر شفاه
Show	عرض
Continuous	متوالٍ
With typed translation	مع ترجمة مطبوعة
Theatre show	عرض (مسرحي)
Browses (surfs) the web	يجول عبر الشبكة العالمية
Pricing	تسعير
Satellite television	تلفاز بقنوات فضائية

SOCIAL ACTIVITIES

Shopping	تسوق
Buys	يشتري/تشتري
Price list	قائمة الأسعار
Goes fishing	يذهب لصيد السمك
Looks for searches	يبحث عن
Birthday	عيد ميلاد
Pocket money	مصروف جيب
Lift	مصعد
Sportsman	رياضي
Ball	كرة
Sports center	مركز رياضي
Sporty, athletic	رياضي
Fishing rod	صنارة صيد السمك
Goes swimming	يذهب/تذهب للسباحة
Goes sledging	يذهب/تذهب للعب بلوح التزلج
Sailing	استخدام المراكب الشراعية
Horse riding	ركوب الخيل
Water skiing	التزلج على الماء

Exercises	يتريّض/تتريّض
Cycling	ركوب الدراجات
Walks	يتمشى/تتمشى
Walks a long distance	يمشي/تمشي لمسافة طويلة
Swims	يسبح/تسبح
Dances	يرقص/ترقص
Relaxes his/her muscles	يرخي عضلاته/ترخي عضلاتها
In the corner	في الزاوية
Cartoon video tape	شريط صور متحركة
Drum	طبل
Well cooked	مطهو جيداً
Hello	أهلاً
Night club	نادي ليلي
Appetizing meal	وجبة شهية
Cheap	رخيص
Party	حفلة
Bottle	زجاجة
Do it yourself	اعمل بنفسك
Bureau de change	مكتب صرافة

Tobacco shop	محل بيع تبغ
Gift	هدية
Box	صندوق
Credit card	بطاقة ائتمان
Shopping center	مركز تسوق
Canned food	أطعمة معلبة
Cheques	شيكات
Expensive	غالي
Choice	خيار
Confectioner	محل حلويات
Penpal	زميل مراسلة
Estimates the cost	يقيم/تقيم الكلفة
Changes (money)	يصرف/تصرف
Chess	شطرنج
Listens to	يستمع/تستمع إلى
Accepts	يقبل/تقبل
Greengrocery	محل بيع الخضر
Team	فريق
Trip abroad tour	جولة خارجية

Saves	يوفر/توفر
Kissing on both cheeks	التقبيل على الوجنتين
Returns to	يعود لِ/تعود لِ
Congratulations	أطيب التمنيات
Closes	يغلق/تغلق
Fireworks	ألعاب نارية
Engagement	خطوبة
Invitation	دعوة
Electronic game	لعبة إلكترونية
Holiday	يوم إجازة
Happy New Year	كل عام وأنتم بخير
Public holiday	عطلة عامة
Delivers a lecture	يحاضر/تحاضر
Reads	يقرأ/تقرأ
Free time	وقت فراغ
Place	محل
Youth club	نادي شباب
Market	سوق
Marriage	زواج

Change	تغيير
Hour	ساعة
Wedding	عرس
Gives a present	يهدي هدية
Opening	افتتاح
Stationery	محل بيع قرطاسية
Easter	عيد الفصح
Perfume	عطر
Hobby	هواية
Cake shop	محل بيع الكعك
Battery	بطارية
Dish of the day	صحن اليوم
Dives	يغوص/تغوص
Size (shoes)	مقاس (الحذاء)
Fishmonger	محل بيع السمك
Wallet	محفظة
Knows	يعرف/تعرف
Happy	مسرور
Department, part	قسم

Looks	ينظر/تنظر
Finds	يجد
Visits	يزور/تزور
Story, novel	رواية
Amuses herself	يتسلّى/تتسلّى
Washes herself	يغتسل/تغتسل
Sunbathes	يتشمس/تتشمس
Rests	يرتاح
Help yourself	اخدم نفسك
Service	خدمة
Reductions, Sales	تنزيلات
Goes out, leaves	يخرج/تخرج
Equipment store	مخزن تجهيزات
Size (clothes)	قياس (للثياب)
Balcony, terrace	شرفة
Shop window	واجهة العرض
Trip	سفرة، رحلة

SOCIAL CONVENTIONS

See you tomorrow	أراك غداً
See you soon	أراك قريباً
Anytime	في أي وقت
Best wishes	مع أطيب التمنيات
Goodbye	مع السلامة
Help	النجدة
Hello	أهلاً
Good night	تصبح/تصبحين على خير
Good evening	مساء الخير
Good morning	صباح الخير
Thank you	شكراً
Sorry	آسف
Hope, wish please	رجاء
Please	من فضلك

PREPOSITIONS

To, towards	إلى
Because of	بسبب
Beside, next to, by, at	إلى جانب
After	بعد
In the end	في النهاية
Approximately	حوالي، تقريباً، نحو
Before	قبل
With	مع
At a certain home	في بيت ما
Opposite	ضد
In	في
From	من
Outside, leaving	خارج
Behind	خلف
Facing	مقابل
On the other hand	من جهة أخرى
Over	فوق
About	حوالي

Until	حتى
Far from	بعيداً عن
During	خلال
Between	بين
Everywhere	في كل مكان
In order to	لكي
Next to, near to	قرب
Without	بدون، من دون
Except	ما عدا
Based on, on the strength of	استناداً إلى
Under	تحت
Over	فوق
In the direction of	باتجاه

ADJECTIVES

Kind	لطيف/لطيفة
Happy	سعيد/سعيدة
Annoying, unpleasant	مزعج/مزعجة
Old, former, prior, past	قديم، سابق
Stupid, silly	غبي
Beautiful, pretty	جميل
Good, fine	جيد
Summary, brief, concise	مختصر
Noisy	ضجيج
Broken	مكسور
Great	عظيم
Comfortable, easy	مريح
Short	قصير
In a good mood	ذو مزاج جيد
Standing, stopping	واقف
Disgusting, repulsive	مقزز
Last	أخير
Sorry	آسف

Amusing	مسلي
Valuable, precious	ثمين
Difficult	صعب
Effective, efficient, active	فعّال
Angry	غاضب
Out, outside	خارج
Weak	ضعيف
Tiring	متعب
Falsified, forged, fake	مزيف
Favorite	مفضل
Closed	مغلق
Locked	مقفل
Wonderful, marvelous	رائع
Strong	قوي
Free	حر
Fat	سمين
High	عالي
Unbelievable, incredulous	لا يصدق
Young, youth	شاب، شباب

Ugly	قبيح
Light	خفيف
Heavy	ثقيل
Funny	مضحك، مسل
Sweet, nice, pretty	حلو
Resembles similar	مشابه، يشابه، تشابه
Mature, ripe	ناضج
Important	مهم
New	جديد
Many, several	كثير العدد
Complete, perfect	كامل
Exciting, inspiring	مثير
Full	مليء
Quickly, in a hurry	في عجلة
Following, next	التالي
Sad	حزين
In demand, required, desired	مطلوب
Grateful, thankful	ممتن
Real	حقيقي

Wise, polite	حكيم، مهذب
True	صحيح
Dirty, unclean	قذر
Moving	مثير للمشاعر
Satisfied, contented	راض
Interested, concerned	مهتم
Strict, inflexible, hard	متشدد
Only, alone, unique, lonely	وحيد
Resident, living, calm, quiet	ساكن
Early	مبكر
Ideal, perfect, exemplary	مثالي
Useful	مفيد
Effective, valid, in operation	ساري المفعول
True, real	صحيح

VERBS

Accompanies	يرافق/ترافق
Lights (up)	يضيء/تضيء
Waits	ينتظر/تنتظر
He has	لديه
She has	لديها
Drinks	يشرب/تشرب
Changes	يغير/تغير
Chooses	يختار/تختار
Understands	يفهم/تفهم
Counts	يعد/تعد
Drives, leads	يقود/تقود
Gets used to	يعتاد/تعتاد على
Believes	يعتقد/تعتقد
Decides	يقرر/تقرر
Asks	يسأل/تسأل
Craves	يشتهي
Wishes	يتمنى، يرغب
Says	يقول/تقول

Argues	يجادل/تجادل
Gives	يعطي/تعطي
Sleeps	ينام/تنام
Writes	يكتب/تكتب
Borrows, takes up a loan	يقترض
Hears	يسمع/تسمع
Enters	يدخل/تدخل
Hopes	يأمل/تأمل
Tries	يحاول/تحاول
Eats	يأكل
Locks	يغلق
Hits a target, is right	يصيب/تصيب
Invites, supplicates God	يدعو/تدعو
Throws	يرمي/ترمي
Leaves	يترك/تترك
Deserves, is worthy of	يستحق/تستحق
Puts	يضع/تضع
Climbs	يتسلق
Appears	يظهر

Opens	يفتح
Forgives, pardons	يعفو
Speaks	يتكلم
Leaves	يترك
Allows	يسمح
Is happy at, is pleased with	يفرح
Cries	يبكي
Pays	يدفع
Is able to, can	يقدر
Travels	يسافر
Suffers	يشقى
Carries	يحمل
Lends	يقرض

DAYS OF THE WEEK

Monday	الاثنين
Tuesday	الثلاثاء
Wednesday	الأربعاء
Thursday	الخميس
Friday	الجمعة
Saturday	السبت
Sunday	الأحد

SEASONS

Spring	الربيع
Summer	الصيف
Autumn	الخريف
Winter	الشتاء

MONTHS OF THE YEAR

January	الشهر الأول: يناير
February	الشهر الثاني: فبراير
March	الشهر الثالث: مارس
April	الشهر الرابع: أبريل
May	الشهر الخامس: مايو
June	الشهر السادس: يونيو
July	الشهر السابع: يوليو
August	الشهر الثامن: أغسطس
September	الشهر التاسع: سبتمبر
October	الشهر العاشر: أكتوبر
November	الشهر الحادي عشر: نوفمبر
December	الشهر الثاني عشر: ديسمبر
Century	قرن
Year	سنة
Month	شهر
Week	أسبوع
Day	يوم

COLOURS

	الجمع	مؤنث	مذكر
blue	زُرق	زَرقاء	أزرَق
red	حُمر	حَمراء	أحمَر
White	بيض	بَيضاء	أبيَض
Black	سُود	سَوداء	أسوَد
Green	خُضر	خَضراء	أخضَر
Yello	صُفر	صَفراء	أصفَر

Brown	بُنّي/ة
Purple	بَنَفسَجيّ/ة
Pink	زَهريّ/ة
Grey	رَماديّ/ة
Gold	ذَهَبيّ/ة
Silver	فضّيّ/ة

	الجمع	مؤنث	مذكر
Dark-complexioned	سُمر	سَمراء	أسمَر
Blond, fair-skinned	شُقر	شَقراء	أشقَر
Grey/white-haired	شيب	شَيباء	أشيَب
Bald	صُلع	صَلعاء	أصلع
Blind	عُمي	عَمياء	أعمى

WEATHER

الشتاء

الخريف

الصيف

الربيع

الجو غائم

مطر/الجو ممطر

ثلج/الجو مثلج

شمس/الجو مشمس

71

ACTIVITIES

كرة القدم

التصوير

التزلج

الموسيقى

الكرة الطائرة

الرسم

السباحة

القراءة

THE BODY

الجِسم

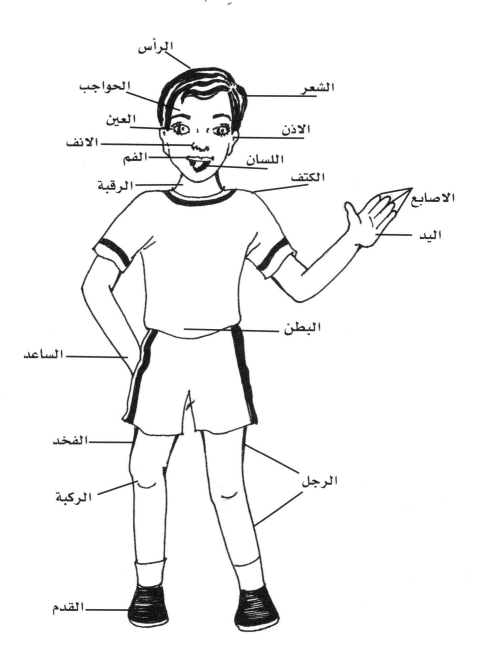

الرأس

الشعر

الحواجب

العين

الاذن

الانف

الفم

اللسان

الرقبة

الكتف

الاصابع

اليد

البطن

الساعد

الفخد

الرجل

الركبة

القدم

FOOD

فاكهة

سمك

دجاج

خضار

أرز

لحم

زيت - ملح- فلفل- خل

شوربة

74

TRANSPORT

سيارة

طائرة

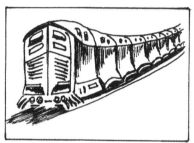
قطار

حافلة/ باص

دراجة نارية

دراجة

مشيا على القدم

سفينة - باخرة

NUMBERS

*	1	واحد
**	2	اثنان
***	3	ثلاثة
****	4	أربعة
*****	5	خمسة
******	6	ستة
*******	7	سبعة
********	8	ثمانية
*********	9	تسعة
**********	10	عشرة
***********	11	أحَد عَشَر
************	12	اثنا عَشَر
*************	13	ثلاثة عشر
**************	14	أربعة عشر
***************	15	خمسة عشر
****************	16	ستة عشر
*****************	17	سبعة عشر
******************	18	ثمانية عشر
*******************	19	تسعة عشر
********************	20	عشرون/عشرين
*********************	21	واحد وعشرون
**********************	22	اثنان وعشرون
***********************	23	ثلاثة وعشرون

76

70	سَبعون/سبعين	30	ثَلاثون/ثلاثين
80	ثَمانون/ثمانين	40	أربَعون/أربعين
90	تِسعون/تسعين	50	خَمسون/خمسين
100	مِئة (مائة)	60	سِتّون/ستّين
600	سِتّمئة	100	مِئة (مائة)
700	سبعمئة	200	مئتان/مئتيْن
800	ثَمانمئة	300	ثلاثمئة
900	تسعمئة	400	أربعمئة
1000	ألف	500	خمسمئة

quarter	رُبع
third	ثُلث
Less (lit.: except)	إلاّ

e.g., 12.55 = الساعة الواحدة إلاّ خمس

minute	دَقيقة ج. دَقائِق
When?	متى...؟
At what time...?	في أيّ ساعة...؟
What is the time...?	كم الساعة...؟

أمثلة: 1.15 الساعة الواحدة والرُبع

5.20 الساعة الخامسة والثُلث

خالد يقول: "جدتي توقظني في الساعة السادسة والنصف".

"أخرج من البيت في العاشرة صباحاً".

مؤنث		مذكر	
السابعة	الأُولى	السّابِع	الأوّل
الثامنة	الثّانية	الثّامن	الثّاني
التاسعة	الثّالثة	التّاسع	الثّالث
العاشرة	الرابعة	العاشر	الرّابع
الحادية عَشَرة	الخامسة	الحادي عَشَر	الخامس
الثانية عَشَرة	السادسة	الثاني عَشَر	السّادِس

1967 (عام) ألف وتسعمئة وسبعة وستّين.

1945 (عام) ألف وتسعمئة وخمسة وأربعين.

1883 (عام) ألف وثمانمئة وثلاثة وثمانين.

1914 (عام) ألف وتسعمئة وأربعة عشر.